◆ THE CIVIL WAR LIBRARY ◆

THE BATTLE OF GETTYSBURG

★ AND ★

LINCOLN'S GETTYSBURG ADDRESS

Carin T. Ford

Enslow Publishers, Inc.

40 Industrial Road   PO Box 38
Box 398   Aldershot
Berkeley Heights, NJ 07922   Hants GU12 6BP
USA   UK

http://www.enslow.com

Library of Congress Cataloging-in-Publication Data

Ford, Carin T.
    The Battle of Gettysburg and Lincoln's Gettysburg Address / Carin T. Ford.
       p. cm. — (The Civil War library)
    Summary: A detailed account of the three days of the Battle of Gettysburg, the bloodiest war fought on American soil, plus an examination of Abraham Lincoln's famous Gettysburg address.
    Includes bibliographical references and index.
    ISBN 0-7660-2253-6 (hardcover)
    1. Gettysburg, Battle of, Gettysburg, Pa., 1863—Juvenile literature. 2. Lincoln, Abraham, 1809–1865. Gettysburg address—Juvenile literature. [1. Gettysburg, Battle of, Gettysburg, Pa., 1863. 2. Lincoln, Abraham, 1809–1865. Gettysburg address. 3. United States—History—Civil War, 1861–1865—Campaigns.] I. Title.
    E475.53.F67 2004
    973.7'349—dc22
                                               2003013723

Printed in the United States of America

10 9 8 7 6 5 4 3 2 1

To Our Readers: We have done our best to make sure all Internet Addresses in this book were active and appropriate when we went to press. However, the author and the publisher have no control over and assume no liability for the material available on those Internet sites or on other Web sites they may link to. Any comments or suggestions can be sent by e-mail to comments@enslow.com or to the address on the back cover.

Every effort has been made to locate all copyright holders of material used in this book. If any errors or omissions have occurred, corrections will be made in future editions of this book.

Illustration Credits: Alexander Gardner, *Photographic Sketch Book of the Civil War* (New York: Dover Publications, Inc., 1959), p. 13; *Authentic Civil War Illustrations*, Dover Publications, Inc., 1995, pp. 2, 6, 7; Carin T. Ford, pp. 20CL, 37 (inset), 39B; Clipart.com, p. 9T, 14C, 14B, 15 (inset), 18–19, 20TL, 27T, 28C, 33R, 34T, 42T; *Dictionary of American Portraits*, Dover Publications, Inc., 1967, pp. 10T, 24T, 39T; *Dictionary of American Portraits*, Dover Publications, Inc., Courtesy of Library of Congress, Brady Collection, pp. 23B, 43BL; Enslow Publishers, Inc., pp. 8B, 14 (map), 20 (map), 28 (map); Kim Widenor, pp. 40L, 41T; Library of Congress, pp. 4–5, 5 (inset), 6–7, 10B, 11, 15 (background), 18, 21 (inset), 23T, 27B, 29 (inset), 30–31, 32T, 32–33B, 40–41, 42B, 42BR, 42TR; National Archives and Records Administration, pp. 9B, 16T, 16B, 19B, 24C, 26B, 31B, 36, 37 (background), 38, 43BR; National Park Service, p. 24B; North Wind Picture Archives, p. 8T, 12, 14TL, 17, 21 (background), 25, 28T, 29 (background), 30B, 35, 43C; Photos.com, pp. 1, 22L.

Cover Illustrations: *Inset*, photos.com. All other cover photos courtesy of the following: Library of Congress; National Archives; Photos.com; Enslow Publishers, Inc.; with the exception of: Song Book, Courtesy National Park Service, Museum Management Program and Gettysburg National Military Park, catalog number GETT31374, www.cr.nps.gov/museum/exhibits/gettex/music2.htm; Patriotic Cover, Courtesy National Park Service, Museum Management Program and Gettysburg National Military Park, catalog number GETT27703, www.cr.nps.gov/museum/exhibits/gettex/write5.htm; Drum carried by Mozart Regiment, Courtesy National Park Service, Museum Management Program and Gettysburg National Military Park, catalog number GETT32847, www.cr.nps.gov/museum/exhibits/gettex/music3.htm; US Flag, Courtesy National Park Service, Museum Management Program and Manassas National Battlefield Park, catalog number MANA979, www.cr.nps.gov/museum/exhibits/flags/mana2.htm.

TABLE OF CONTENTS

CHAPTER ONE

INVADING THE NORTH

Joshua Chamberlain did not know what to do. It was July 2, 1863—the second day of the fighting in Gettysburg, Pennsylvania. Chamberlain was leader of the 20th Maine Infantry in the Union army. He had been ordered to hold a hill called Little Round Top at all costs. He could not let the Confederates take control of it.

Chamberlain had fewer than 400 soldiers. Most of them were fishermen and lumberjacks. They had no experience in battle. But they were stubborn and willing to fight to the death. Five times the Confederates tried to push them off the hill. Five times they pushed the Confederates back.

"The blood stood in puddles in some places on the rocks," said Confederate colonel William Oates.[1]

The bodies of soldiers who had been killed or wounded lay everywhere. Chamberlain had lost a third of his men after an hour and a half of fighting. The rest of the soldiers had only a few bullets left for their guns. Chamberlain's men could not give up the hill . . . yet how could they stay and fight without bullets?

Suddenly he yelled, "Bayonet!"[2] Each man quickly jammed a steel blade into the muzzle end of his gun. The Maine soldiers then charged wildly down the hill with their bayonets held high—straight at the terrified Southerners.

A bayonet is a sword stuck into a rifle.

Chamberlain's plan worked. The Confederates ran away "like a herd of wild cattle," said Oates.[3] The Union had held Little Round Top.

❧

The Battle of Gettysburg lasted three days. It took place halfway through the Civil War. The war had started in April 1861, but trouble had been brewing between the Northern and Southern states for years. At the root of the problem was slavery. For 250 years, slaves had worked on Southern farms and plantations. Slaves planted and harvested the cotton that made money for the South.

Slaves often worked fourteen hours a day in the hot fields. They were not paid. They were treated like property. Many were harshly beaten, and few had enough to eat.

The businesses and small farms of the North did not depend on slaves to do the work.

Thousands of men died on Little Round Top.

WHO'S WHO IN
THE CIVIL WAR

❖ The North was also known as the Union, or the United States. The people there were often called Yankees.

❖ The South was called the Confederacy, or the Confederate States. During the war, Southerners were also called Rebels or Johnny Reb.

Slavery had been abolished—or ended—in the North years earlier. Many Northerners believed slavery was wrong.

Southerners did not want to get rid of slavery. They worried that President Lincoln, a Northerner, would try to end slavery throughout the United States. Southerners did not think the federal government had the right to tell each state what to do.

The South needed slaves to grow cotton.

THE UNION AND THE CONFEDERACY

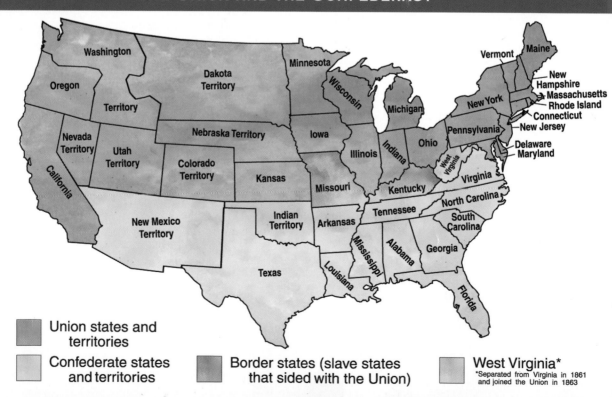

Union states and territories

Confederate states and territories

Border states (slave states that sided with the Union)

West Virginia*
*Separated from Virginia in 1861 and joined the Union in 1863

Beginning in December 1860, seven Southern states broke away—or seceded—from the rest of the country. They formed their own country, the Confederate States of America. They set up their own government. But President Lincoln was determined to keep the United States together.

The Civil War began with the attack on Fort Sumter.

Confederate soldiers fired on Union soldiers on April 12, 1861, at Fort Sumter, South Carolina. Soon after, four more states joined the Confederacy. The Civil War began as a battle to bring these states back into the United States, or Union.

Many Northerners thought it would be a short war. They had more men and more guns. Yet during the first two years of fighting, the South won many victories over the Northern soldiers.

This Confederate soldier, Edmund Ruffin, fired the first shot of the war.

Part of the reason was Robert E. Lee. A polite man in his mid-fifties with a neat white beard, Lee was the chief general of the Confederate armies. He was an excellent military leader, and his men were devoted to him.

By 1863, Lee was eager to invade the North. He came from Virginia, where there had been a lot of fighting.

Lee hoped to draw the fighting away from his war-torn state. Also, Confederate soldiers would be able to find badly needed food and supplies in the North. Finally, Lee believed that most Northerners were getting tired of the war. He thought that if the South won a major victory in the North, Northerners might want to end the war and make peace with the Confederacy.

In June 1863, Lee led 75,000 men up to central

Jeb Stuart was one of the youngest and bravest generals in the war.

◆ ROBERT E. LEE ◆

Robert E. Lee graduated with the second highest grades in his class at West Point Military Academy. In early 1861, President Lincoln asked Lee to take command of the Union army. It was a hard decision for Lee. He did not believe in slavery. He also did not think the South should have broken away from the rest of the nation. Still, he would not fight against his home state of Virginia.

"If Virginia stands by the old Union, so will I," he said. "But if she secedes . . . then I will follow my native State with my sword, and if need be with my life."[4]

Lee said no to President Lincoln. Instead, he joined the Confederate army.

Pennsylvania. General James E. B. "Jeb" Stuart rode ahead of Lee. Stuart led the cavalry—the soldiers on horseback. His job was to scout the area and find out exactly where the Union army was located. Stuart decided to ride around the entire Union army so he could give General Lee a full report.

The Union forces were led by General George G. Meade. Meade had just been made the Union commander a couple of days earlier. He had a quick temper and a sharp tongue. Soldiers did not always like Meade, but they respected him.[5]

"I am moving at once against Lee . . . and will settle this thing one way or the other," Meade wrote to his wife.[6]

The Union army was made up of 95,000 men. They were spread out over many miles, and it took Stuart longer than he expected to ride around them. Stuart was not able to get word to Lee about the Union

General Lee worried about Stuart: **"I ought to have heard from him long before now."**[7]

11

army's position. So General Lee had no idea where the Union army was—or how big it was.

On July 1, Lee's soldiers were just west of Gettysburg, Pennsylvania. It was a hot, sticky day in the hilly farm town, where peaches and wheat grew.[8] Gettysburg was a small town of only 2,400 people. Lee had heard that his soldiers would be able to get shoes there; they needed them badly.[9]

While Lee's men marched, some Union cavalry were scouting the area, looking for Confederate soldiers. In the early hours of the morning, the two groups ran into each other. Fighting broke out on a long hill called McPherson Ridge.

Both sides called quickly for extra help. Soon it arrived: 25,000 Confederate soldiers and 19,000 Union soldiers. The Confederates were able to push the Union troops through the streets of Gettysburg and south of town.

"People were running here and there screaming that the town would be shelled," said Sallie Broadhead, who lived in

Gettysburg. "No one knew where to go or what to do."[10]

By nightfall, Lee had lost about 6,500 men. In the Union army, 12,000 soldiers were killed, wounded, or missing.

The Confederates had won the first day of the battle. Yet Meade was pleased with the Union army's position for the following day of fighting. His men were spread out on Culp's Hill and Cemetery Hill. On the high ground, they could easily see the position of the Confederate soldiers. They were ready to fight them off if there was an attack.

The first day of the battle was over. Lee's men were north and west of town. Lee had not yet heard from Stuart. He still did not know where the rest of the Union troops were, nor how many men there were. But he was determined to continue fighting. "I am going to whip them," he said, "or they are going to whip me."[11]

This picture of the town of Gettysburg was taken from Cemetery Ridge, after the Union soldiers made camp.

13

DAY 1 AT GETTYSBURG: JULY 1, 1863

Carlisle Road

Heidlersburg Road

Mummasburg Road

Unfinished Railroad

Chambersburg Pike

Gettysburg and Hanover Railroad

York Pike

GETTYSBURG

Hanover Road

McPHERSON WOODS

McPHERSON RIDGE

SEMINARY RIDGE

Hagerstown Road

CEMETERY HILL

CULP'S HILL

Rock Creek

Emmitsburg Road

CEMETERY RIDGE

Baltimore Pike

PEACH ORCHARD

WHEAT FIELD

DEVIL'S DEN

LITTLE ROUND TOP

Taneytown Road

N
W   E
S

Confederate lines
Union lines

Confederate soldiers burned the barn at McPherson Farm.

LEE'S HEADQUARTERS

MEADE'S HEADQUARTERS

The Confederate soldiers attacked the Union cavalry on McPherson Ridge, west of town. By 4 P.M., the Union soldiers were overpowered, and many were captured.

SECOND DAY
OF BATTLE

July 2, 1863, was a cloudy, hot Thursday. Soldiers had arrived throughout the night, making both armies stronger. Lee was eager to attack, although his 65,000 Confederate soldiers would be up against 85,000 Union men. Lee knew he faced a hard task. Yet he did not believe anyone could defeat his army.[1]

Many different battles would take place that day. Lee's main goal was to take the hilly region south of Gettysburg—Little Round Top and Big Round Top.

General James Longstreet led the Confederate attack. He was supposed to start early in the day, but it took him until late afternoon to move his men into position.

Union general Daniel F. Sickles had been ordered by Meade to hold Little Round Top. But Sickles did not like this position. He decided instead to move his troops half a mile forward to high open ground near a peach orchard.[2]

Meade was very angry when he learned what Sickles had done. Now there was no one to defend the Round Tops. Meade ordered Sickles back to Little Round Top, but there was no time. The Confederates had begun their attack.

General Lee called General Longstreet, right, his "war horse."

The fighting was fierce. Meade was as determined as Lee. He quickly sent four regiments to the hill. Longstreet was able to break through the Union line, but his attack was stopped as more Union soldiers arrived at Little Round Top.

The 20th Maine Infantry was the last to arrive. The struggle was bloody. First Lieutenant Charles E. Hazlett was standing near another Union officer, who was suddenly shot in the head. Hazlett leaned forward to catch the dying man's words. Suddenly he, too, was shot and fell dead on top of

Longstreet aimed his artillery at the Round Tops.

Longstreet
and his men
attacked
the Union
soldiers on
Cemetery
Ridge.

the officer. There were many deaths on both sides. But the Union soldiers held on to Little Round Top.

In the peach orchard, Sickles's men were involved in another terrible battle. During the fighting, Sickles was hit by a cannonball. Although his right leg was shattered, the general stayed calm. He smoked a cigar as he was carried from the field.

More soldiers arrived to help Sickles's men fight in the orchard, the wheat field, and Devil's Den.

To the north of these battle sites, the Confederates tried to take Cemetery Ridge and Cemetery Hill. But Union soldiers were able to fight them off.

By the end of the second day of the battle, the Confederates had won some ground at Culp's Hill. Yet the Union lines still held strong. The fighting had been so brutal, it was said that the water in Plum Run stream flowed blood red.[3] People later called this area the Valley of Death. Each army had lost about 9,000 men.

Lee and Meade met with their officers that night. They made plans for the next day. So far, the Confederates had attacked the Union army on both its sides . . . and failed.

Meade turned to General John Gibbon, who commanded the troops on Cemetery Ridge, at the center of the Union line. "If Lee attacks tomorrow," Meade said, "it will be in your front."[5]

Sickles was so badly wounded that he had to have his leg cut off, like this soldier. Sickles packed the leg in a small coffin and kept it with him for much of his life.[4]

Fighting was brutal at Culp's Hill.

Devil's Den was steep and rocky, adding to the difficulty of the fighting there.

McPHERSON WOODS

Unfinished Railroad

Chambersburg Pike

Gettysburg and Hanover Railroad

York Pike

Hanover Road

GETTYSBURG

McPHERSON RIDGE

SEMINARY RIDGE

Hagerstown Road

CEMETERY HILL

CULP'S HILL

Rock Creek

Emmitsburg Road

CEMETERY RIDGE

Baltimore Pike

PEACH ORCHARD

WHEAT FIELD

Taneytown Road

DEVIL'S DEN

VALLEY OF DEATH

LITTLE ROUND TOP

Plum Run

BIG ROUND TOP

N
W   E
S

Confederate lines
Union lines

The Confederates attacked Meade's army on the left and the right, but the Union held on to its strong positions. The Confederates gained part of Culp's Hill, but nothing more.

CHAPTER THREE

PICKETT'S CHARGE

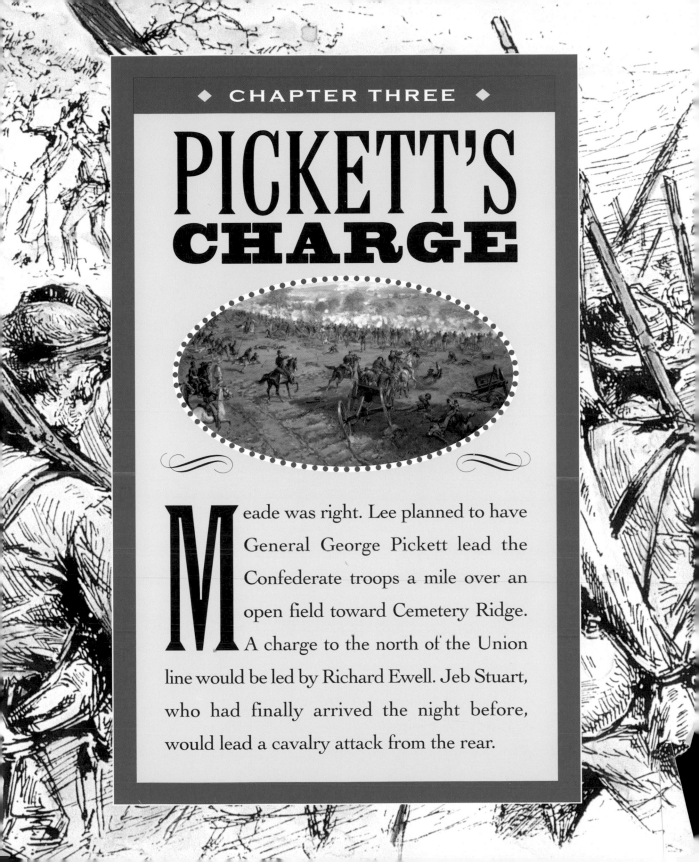

Meade was right. Lee planned to have General George Pickett lead the Confederate troops a mile over an open field toward Cemetery Ridge. A charge to the north of the Union line would be led by Richard Ewell. Jeb Stuart, who had finally arrived the night before, would lead a cavalry attack from the rear.

The three attacks were supposed to take place at the same time. Yet it was hours before Pickett could get his men into position. Meanwhile, Ewell charged Culp's Hill at four o'clock in the morning. For seven hours, the Confederates fought boldly. At last, they were driven back.

Next came Pickett. He was a dashing Virginian who wore his hair in ringlets. He had graduated from West Point Military Academy with the lowest grades in his class. On that hot and sticky Friday, Pickett believed he would be able to smash through the center of the Union line.

Not everyone thought Lee's plan was a good one. General Longstreet had tried to talk Lee out of it. The 15,000 Confederate soldiers would have little protection as they marched over the wide-open field. Plus, the Union had gotten more men and more ammunition during the night. Their position on the high ground of Cemetery Ridge was strong.

"I have been a soldier all my life," Longstreet told Lee. "It is my opinion that no 15,000 men . . . can take that position."[1]

But Lee would not change his mind. "The enemy is there and I am going to strike him" he said.[2]

Confederate cannons began blasting the Union line around 1 P.M. But all they did was to damage some farmland and fill the area with smoke. The Union then set off its own cannons.

After nearly two hours, the firing stopped.[3] Pickett was eager to begin his charge. He looked at Longstreet, waiting for the command. But Longstreet was

Confederate general Pickett, below, led his men in a hopeless charge across an open field.

too upset to speak. He was certain the attack would fail. He just nodded his head.

"Up men, and to your posts!" Pickett shouted. "Don't forget today that you are from old Virginia."[4]

Armistead, top, and Hancock were good friends before the Civil War put them on opposite sides of the fight.

The 15,000 Confederate soldiers began marching across the field.

The Union soldiers were waiting on the hill behind a stone wall. They watched the Confederates approach.

◆ FRIEND AGAINST FRIEND ◆

Confederate general Lewis A. Armistead and Union general Winfield Scott Hancock had been friends for nearly twenty years. They were forced to lead their men against each other at Gettysburg. Before the Confederate attack on Cemetery Ridge, Armistead said that if he died in battle, he wanted his Bible to be sent to Hancock's wife.

During Pickett's Charge, Armistead was shot. As he lay on the field, he handed a Union soldier his watch and valuables and asked him to give a message to General Hancock. "Tell General Hancock for me that I have done him and done you all an injury which I shall regret the longest day I live."[5]

As it turned out, Hancock, too, was wounded in the battle that day. He recovered, but Armistead died two days later. Today, a monument called "Friend to Friend" honors these men at Gettysburg National Military Park. It shows Armistead handing his watch to a soldier.

Many Union soldiers were filled with wonder and admiration. Pickett's charge was courageous . . . and hopeless.

As soon as the Confederates came closer, the Union guns shot down row after row of soldiers. Often, ten Southerners were killed by a single exploding artillery shell.

"We could not help hitting them at every shot," said one Union officer.[6]

A few Confederates briefly made it to the wall. Yet all who did were killed or captured. A Union soldier named Micah said, "What men are these we slaughter like cattle and still they come at us?"[7]

Pickett watched as more than half his unit fell, nearly 7,000 soldiers. He finally ordered his men to retreat.

Lee then ordered Pickett to gather his

On the open field, Pickett's men made easy targets for the Union soldiers. They were gunned down as they reached the Union center.

25

THE ONE
CIVILIAN DEATH

❖ On the morning of July 3, 1863, Jennie Wade of Gettysburg was baking bread. Her sister had a new baby boy, and Jennie had come to help out. Jennie was kneading dough at her sister's kitchen table when a bullet pierced the door and hit her in the back. She was killed instantly.

❖ Jennie was the only citizen of Gettysburg to be killed in the battle. She was twenty years old.

division of men and prepare for an attack by the Union. Pickett said, "General Lee, I *have* no division now."[8] Pickett was miserable about the deaths of his men. "The moans of my wounded boys, the sight of the dead, upturned faces flood my soul with grief," Pickett wrote.[9]

Lee took full blame for the failed attack. "It's all my fault," he said. He had believed that his men could not be beaten.[10]

The attack became known as Pickett's Charge. It was the end of the Battle of Gettysburg. The Confederate army never again invaded the North.

The cavalry attack, led by Jeb Stuart, failed, too. The soldiers tried to go behind Union lines and attack from the rear. But they were stopped by Union cavalry, led by the young general George Armstrong Custer.

Custer was called the "Boy General" because he was only twenty-three years old.

Although the Union army had won the battle, both sides had lost many men. In the Northern army, 23,000 soldiers were killed, wounded, missing, or captured. The South had lost almost 28,000 men—one third of Lee's army.

That evening, a Union soldier wrote in his diary, "If ever I was glad to have night come I am tonight."[11]

The Union cavalry, left, held off the Confederate calvary attack.

Many men on both sides of the war, like this Union soldier, dreamed of returning home to their wives and children.

27

Pickett's Charge

The Union cavalry

DAY 3 AT GETTYSBURG: JULY 3, 1863

Unfinished Railroad

Chambersburg Pike

Gettysburg and Hanover Railroad

York Pike

Hanover Road

GETTYSBURG

McPHERSON RIDGE

SEMINARY RIDGE

CEMETERY HILL

CULP'S HILL

CEMETERY RIDGE

Rock Creek

Cavalry battle took place 3 miles east→

Emmitsburg Road

PEACH ORCHARD

WHEAT FIELD

Taneytown Road

Custer's cavalry

Stuart's cavalry

DEVIL'S DEN

VALLEY OF DEATH

LITTLE ROUND TOP

Plum Run

BIG ROUND TOP

N
W E
S

Confederate lines

Union lines

Pickett's Charge was a disaster, and the Battle of Gettysburg was over.

CHAPTER FOUR

AFTER THE BATTLE

The next day was the Fourth of July. General Lee pulled his soldiers out of Pennsylvania, and they began walking home in the rain to Virginia. His army was in no shape to fight. Still, Lee made sure they were ready in case Union soldiers came after them.

But Meade did not follow Lee into the

During the three-day battle, the townsfolk of Gettysburg hid in their cellars or ran away to nearby towns. Finally, the defeated Confederate soldiers began their retreat.

South. His men were tired, and they had just about run out of food. Meade was content with winning the battle and pushing the Confederates off Northern land.

President Lincoln was furious that Meade did not go after Lee. "Will our generals never get the idea out of their heads?" he asked. "The whole country is our soil."[1]

If Meade had attacked and defeated the Confederates, the Civil War might have ended then. Instead, the fighting dragged on for two more years.

The three-day battle had left the town of Gettysburg

in shambles. Crops were destroyed, property was damaged, food was stolen, and houses were robbed. The fields were now covered with thousands of wounded and dead soldiers. The dead bodies were piled one on top of another.

"The houses, the barns, the sheds, and the open barnyards were crowded with moaning and wailing human beings . . . ," said Union general Carl Schurz. "I saw long rows of men lying under the eaves of the buildings, the [rain] water pouring down their bodies in streams."[2] The fields of Gettysburg were also covered with the bodies of 5,000 dead horses.

It was left to the townsfolk to take the wounded soldiers into their homes, schools, and churches. Tables were quickly set up so doctors could operate on the men. In the fields, blankets were draped over poles to make tents to keep out the rain.

Burying dead soldiers was a gruesome job.

Three Confederate prisoners from the Battle of Gettysburg.

At that time, little was known about medicine or germs. Surgeons often held their knives between their teeth as they prepared to cut off the arms or legs of hundreds of wounded men.

The citizens of Gettysburg, along with hired workers and captured Confederate soldiers, also faced the task of burying the 8,000 dead soldiers. It was a huge job. The bodies were pushed into open ditches, sometimes hundreds at a time. When a soldier's name was known, it was written on a wooden marker and placed near him.

Several days after the battle, Pennsylvania's governor, Andrew G. Curtin, traveled to Gettysburg. He was shocked by the terrible sights and smells.

Curtin decided to buy land so the men who died in the battle could be properly

John Burns lived in the town of Gettysburg. He took out his gun and joined the Union soldiers in battle. Burns fought bravely and was wounded three times.

A new cemetery was designed to honor the fallen soldiers at Gettysburg.

32

buried. He put David Wills, a lawyer, in charge. Wills bought some land on the northern slope of Cemetery Hill. It would be divided into different areas for the men of different states.

Wills planned a ceremony to dedicate the cemetery. He invited some famous writers of the day to speak, including poet Henry Wadsworth Longfellow.[3] None were able to attend.

Wills then asked Edward Everett to give a speech. Everett was an important man. In the past, he had been the governor of Massachusetts, a U.S. senator, and the president of Harvard University. About five weeks later, Wills also wrote to President Lincoln, asking if he would come and make "a few . . . remarks."[4]

The ceremony was seventeen days away. This did not give Lincoln much time to write a speech. He made some notes on a piece of paper. There were only eight

Here, in the Wills House, Lincoln put the finishing touches on his Gettysburg Address.

sentences. When he penciled in a ninth sentence, he needed another piece of paper.

Lincoln made the six-hour trip to Gettysburg on November 18. Traveling with him were several government workers, some army and navy officers, and his friend Ward Lamon.

On the train ride, Lincoln talked with the other men for an hour, then said, "Gentlemen, this is all very pleasant, but the people will expect me to say something to them tomorrow, and I must give the matter some thought."[5] He finished making changes to his speech that night at the home of David Wills.

The ceremony took place the next day in front of thousands of people. There was fog and some rain. Yet the area was filled with tables at which people were selling cookies, lemonade, and souvenirs of the battle. Visitors could buy canteens, soldiers' buttons, and dead wildflowers from the battlefield.

Wearing a new black suit and black stovepipe hat, Lincoln sat on the wooden platform. He did not feel well; he had a fever.

Everett arrived late. He was the main speaker, and he talked for two hours. He used fancy words to describe the fighting of the past two years. He carefully told the details of each day of the Gettysburg battle. As Everett was finishing, Lincoln took a piece of paper out of his pocket and silently read it through.

The audience clapped loudly for Everett. Then a chorus sang a hymn for the dead

People have described Lincoln's voice as high and shrill. It was not always pleasant, but it was easy to hear.[6]

soldiers. As Lincoln stood up, a photographer began to set up his camera.

Lincoln started his speech, making some changes as he spoke.[7] A little more than two minutes later, he was done. Many historians say that the audience was so surprised, they barely clapped. The photographer had not even had time to get the cap off his camera lens.[8] Other historians say his speech was interrupted many times by applause.[9]

In fact, there is no picture of Lincoln delivering the Gettysburg Address. None of the newspaper reporters had time to take notes.

The president unhappily sat down. "It is a flat failure and the people are disappointed," he said to his friend Lamon.[10]

This blurry picture is the only known photograph taken of President Lincoln at Gettysburg.

CHAPTER FIVE

REMEMBRANCE

On the evening of November 19, 1863, Lincoln took the train back to Washington, D.C. He was tired and ill. Lincoln lay down on his seat with a wet towel across his eyes.

The following day, Everett's speech made the front pages of the newspapers. Lincoln's speech was printed on the inside pages.

Lincoln spoke from the heart in his Gettysburg Address.

Four score and seven years ago, our fathers brought forth on this continent, a new nation, conceived in liberty, and dedicated to the proposition that all men are created equal.

Now we are engaged in a great civil war, testing whether that nation, or any nation so conceived and so dedicated, can long endure. We are met on a great battle-field of that war. We have come to dedicate a portion of that field, as a final resting place for those who here gave their lives that the nation might live. It is altogether fitting and proper that we should do this.

But, in a larger sense, we cannot dedicate—we cannot consecrate—we cannot hallow—this ground. The brave men, living and dead, who struggled here, have consecrated it, far above our poor power to add or detract. The world will little note, nor long remember what we say here, but it can never forget what they did here. It is for us the living, rather, to be dedicated here to the unfinished work which they who fought here have thus far so nobly advanced. It is rather for us to be here dedicated to the great task remaining before us—that from these honored dead we take increased devotion to that cause for which they gave the last full measure of devotion—that we here highly resolve that these dead shall not have died in vain—that this nation, under God, shall have a new birth of freedom, and that government of the people, by the people, for the people, shall not perish from the earth.

Although many newspapers praised the speech, the London *Times* said Lincoln was "dull and commonplace."[1] The Chicago *Times* called his speech "silly."[2]

Today, it has become one of the most famous speeches in the nation's history.

Lincoln's speech contained about 270 words. He said the nation should live up to the idea that "all men are created equal." The Civil War was a test. Could a government based on treating all people equally survive?[3]

Edward Everett admired Lincoln's speech.

Lincoln did not mention any person by name in his speech. He did not talk about slavery, the Union, or the Confederacy. He did not even mention Gettysburg.[4] Lincoln spoke about honoring the men who had died. He said they gave their lives to keep the United States together as one nation. Gettysburg stood for a new birth of freedom throughout the nation.

Mass graves hold the many unknown soldiers who died in the Civil War.

Today, many monuments honor the memory of soldiers from the Union and the Confederacy who gave their lives in this terrible battle.

Everett liked the president's speech. He told Lincoln that he wished he had spoken as well "in two hours as you did in two minutes."[5]

When Lincoln gave the Gettysburg Address, only a part of the cemetery had been finished. It was hard finding out the names of all the men who had died. More than 1,600 soldiers could not be named. They were buried as unknown soldiers. The cemetery was finally finished on March 18, 1864.

The loss at Gettysburg was a blow to the Confederacy. It became even weaker when Confederate soldiers surrendered to Union soldiers at Vicksburg, Mississippi, on July 4. Port Hudson, Louisiana, fell several days later. Then the Union controlled the Mississippi River. The Confederacy had been split in half.

The Civil War came to an end in the spring of 1865. On April 9, General Lee surrendered to Union general Ulysses S. Grant in Appomattox, Virginia. Soon after, the rest of the Confederate armies laid down their weapons.

The Battle of Gettysburg is the most famous battle

The Battle of Gettysburg was the turning point of the Civil War. The South never regained its strength.

in American history.[6] More than a million people visit Gettysburg each year. There they can see the statues and monuments that honor the men from the North and the South who gave their lives for their beliefs.

Civil War reenactments are often held on the battlefield at Gettysburg.

THE BATTLE OF GETTYSBURG ★AND★ LINCOLN'S GETTYSBURG ADDRESS TIMELINE

1861

Shots are fired at Fort Sumter; Civil War begins.

Four more Southern states secede.

1862

Battle between two ironclad ships, *Monitor* and *Merrimack*.

Robert E. Lee becomes commander of the Confederate army.

1863

May 15, Lee plans invasion of the North.

ROBERT E. LEE

1860	1861	1862

1860

Abraham Lincoln is elected president.

South Carolina secedes from the United States.

1861

Six more Southern states secede; the Confederacy is formed.

1861

The Union is defeated at 1st Battle of Bull Run.

1862

The Union is defeated at 2nd Battle of Bull Run.

Union victory at Antietam.

Lincoln issues Emancipation Proclamation.

1863

June 3, Lee's army marches northward.

1863
June 28,
Meade
takes over
Army of the
Potomac.

1863
July 2,
Union lines
remain strong;
20th Maine
holds Little
Round Top.

1863
July 4,
Lee's army
heads back to
Virginia.

1864
Ulysses S.
Grant is named
commander
of the Union
army.

William T.
Sherman
captures
Atlanta for
the Union.

1865
Petersburg
and Richmond
fall to the
Union.

Confederate
general
Robert E. Lee
surrenders to
Union general
Ulysses S.
Grant.

1863   **1864**   **1865**

1863
July 1,
Battle of
Gettysburg
begins with
fighting on
the outskirts
of town.

GEORGE PICKETT

1863
July 3,
Pickett's
Charge fails;
Battle of
Gettysburg
ends in
Union victory.

1863
July 4 and 9,
Grant captures
Vicksburg and
then Port
Hudson for the
Union. The
Confederacy is
split in two.

1864
Sherman begins
his "March to
the Sea."

Lincoln is
reelected for
another term
as president.

1865
President
Lincoln is
assassinated.

ABRAHAM LINCOLN

Andrew
Johnson
becomes
president.

≈ Words to Know ≈

address — A speech.

ammunition — Bullets or other explosives shot from guns or cannons.

Confederate States of America — The new nation formed by eleven Southern states in 1861 (also called the Confederacy). These states were South Carolina, Alabama, Florida, Mississippi, Louisiana, Texas, Georgia, Virginia, Arkansas, Tennessee, and North Carolina.

dedicate — To show to the public for the first time. To set apart for a special use.

federal — The central government of a union of states.

line — Military troops arranged side by side.

reenactment — The acting out of events of the past.

retreat — Withdrawal of military troops from a dangerous situation.

secede — To withdraw or break away from.

shell — A hollow tube that holds explosives.

West Point Military Academy — A military school started in 1802 to train men to be army officers. (Starting in 1976, women could attend, too.)

Chapter Notes

CHAPTER 1.
Invading the North

1. Shelby Foote, *The Civil War: A Narrative. Fredericksburg to Meridian* (New York: Random House, 1963), p. 504.
2. Noah Andre Trudeau, *Gettysburg: A Testing of Courage* (New York: HarperCollins Publishers, 2002), p. 370.
3. Geoffrey C. Ward, *The Civil War: An Illustrated History* (New York: Knopf, 1990), p. 221.
4. Winston S. Churchill, *The Great Republic: A History of America* (New York: Modern Library, 2000), p. 151.
5. A. Wilson Greene and Gary W. Gallagher, *National Geographic Guide to the Civil War: National Battlefield Parks* (Washington, D.C.: National Geographic Society, 1992), p. 81.
6. Howard K. Pfanz, *Gettysburg: The First Day* (Chapel Hill, North Carolina: The University of North Carolina Press, 2001), p. 43.
7. Foote, p. 474.
8. Weather reports for the three days of battle come from <http://home.epix. net/~rplr/gettys1.htm.> (June 27, 2003).
9. Pfanz, p. 51.
10. Ward, p. 216.
11. Foote, p. 480.

CHAPTER 2.
Second Day of Battle

1. William K. Kingaman, *Abraham Lincoln and the Road to Emancipation* (New York: Viking, 2001), p. 258.
2. Gary W. Gallagher, ed., *Three Days at Gettysburg* (Kent, Ohio: Kent State University Press, 1999), p. 140.
3. <http://home.epix.net/~rplr/gettys2. htm> (June 27, 2003).
4. Noah Andre Trudeau, *Gettysburg: A Testing of Courage* (New York: HarperCollins Publishers, 2002), p. 417.
5. Shelby Foote, *The Civil War: A Narrative. Fredericksburg to Meridian* (New York: Random House, 1963), p. 525.

CHAPTER 3.
Pickett's Charge

1. Edward J. Stackpole, *They Met at Gettysburg* (Harrisburg, Pa.: Stackpole Books, 1956), p. 245.
2. Charles Carleton Coffin, *Eyewitness to Gettysburg* (Thorndike, Maine: G.K. Hall & Co., 1997), p. 149, Large Print.
3. Shelby Foote, *The Civil War: A Narrative. Fredericksburg to Meridian* (New York: Random House, 1963), p. 549.
4. Geoffrey C. Ward, *The Civil War: An Illustrated History* (New York: Knopf, 1990), p. 228.
5. <http://home.epix.net/~rplr/gettys3.htm> (June 27, 2003).
6. Ward, p. 232.

7. Jeffrey D. Wert, *Gettysburg: Day Three* (New York: Simon & Schuster, 2001), p. 302.
8. Ward, p. 236.
9. Arthur Crew Inman, ed., *Soldier of the South: General Pickett's War Letters to His Wife* (Temecula, Calif.: Reprint Services Corp., 1928).
10. Foote, p. 569.
11. Wert, p. 287.

CHAPTER 4.
After the Battle

1. Bruce Catton, *Gettysburg: The Final Fury* (New York: Doubleday, 1974), p. 101.
2. <http://www.civilwarhome.com/fieldsurgeons.htm> (June 27, 2003).
3. Garry Wills, *Lincoln at Gettysburg: The Words that Remade America* (New York: Simon & Schuster, 1992), p. 23.
4. <http://www.loc.gov/exhibits/gadd/gainv1.html> (June 27, 2003).
5. Shelby Foote, *The Civil War: A Narrative. Fredericksburg to Meridian* (New York: Random House, 1963), p. 830.
6. Wills, p. 36.
7. William K. Kingaman, *Abraham Lincoln and the Road to Emancipation* (New York: Viking, 2001) p. 271.
8. Foote, 832.
9. Wills, p. 36.
10. Foote, p. 832.

CHAPTER 5.
Remembrance

1. Geoffrey C. Ward, *The Civil War: An Illustrated History* (New York: Knopf, 1990), p. 262.
2. Shelby Foote, *The Civil War: A Narrative. Fredericksburg to Meridian* (New York: Random House, 1963), p. 832.
3. Kent Gramm, *November: Lincoln's Elegy at Gettysburg* (Bloomington, Indiana: Indiana University Press, 2001), pp. 136–137.
4. Garry Wills, *Lincoln at Gettysburg: The Words that Remade America* (New York: Simon & Schuster, 1992), p. 37.
5. <http://www.americaslibrary.gov/cgi-big/page.cgi/jb/civil/gettysbg-3.htm> (June 27, 2003).
6. A.Wilson Greene and Gary W. Gallagher, *National Geographic Guide to the Civil War: National Battlefield Parks* (Washington, D.C.: National Geographic Society, 1992), p. 80.

Learn More

BOOKS

Burgan, Michael. *The Battle of Gettysburg*. Minneapolis, Minn.: Compass Point Books, 2001.

Cooper, Jason. *Gettysburg*. Vero Beach, Fla.: Rourke Corp., 1999.

Feinberg, Barbara Silberdick. *Abraham Lincoln's Gettysburg Address: Four Score and More*. Broookfield, Conn.: Twenty-First Century Books, 2000.

Herbert, Janis. *The Civil War for Kids*. Chicago, Ill.: Chicago Review Press, 1999,

INTERNET ADDRESSES

The Battle of Gettysburg
   <http://www.civilwarhome.com/gettysbu.htm>

National Park Service: Gettysburg National Military Park.
The Story of the Battle of Gettysburg
   <http://www.nps.gov/getttour/main-ms.htm>

The Battle of Gettysburg
   <http://brotherswar.com>

Index

Pages numbers for photographs are in **boldface** type.